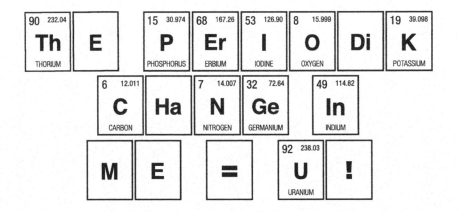

Dr. Donovan Thompson

ISBN (Print): 978-1-09833-773-5
ISBN (eBook): 978-1-09833-774-2

For Tomeka, the change in me.........

WHO AM I?

My name is Donovan Thompson and I am from Savannah, Georgia. Currently, I am in my early thirties and I am married to Tomeka Thompson (she is a Jersey native). I have three brothers (I am a fraternal twin) and my parents, Tony and Cora Thompson, are still thankfully living. I grew up under a Christian household where rules exist, chores were giving out to each of us (and made sure we completed them), and education was highly valued. Both of my parents are college educated. Also, my brothers and I are all college graduates because my parents preached about going to college. Not to limit it to that, my mother drilled into our heads to have morals and standards; and a mind to think. Her words use to be, "thinking sets you apart and it allows you to have autonomy over your thoughts, dreams, aspirations, and goals."

I took those teachings, and others, to heart so I always strived to achieve all I could, even if it was faced with hardship. Reading has always been a part of my DNA because it enabled me to learn new things, expand my vocabulary, and helped with writing. In grade school, I won an award for reading the most books of my grade level and as a child I used to ask for books and encyclopedias as gifts from my parents. They, of course, thought it was weird, given the fact that my siblings wanted toys, games, and other gifts typically wanted by children. That intellectual pursuit never stopped so I graduated from high school in the top 10% of my class (the male with the highest GPA). I also obtained my Bachelors, Masters, and Ph.D. in Chemistry. Thus far, that long scholastic journey was the hardest, but I would not trade it for the world. It was such a rich experience because I learned about many cultures (I traveled internationally and domestically during that time and I still enjoy traveling for work and pleasure), figured out my true learning style (which is through application), my chemistry understanding and the relation it has on everyday life was strengthened, and how to commit myself to something you really want (in this case to be called Dr. Thompson). Throughout all of this, not only was reading and learning very enjoyable, I also found a love for writing. This is very important in my current career. I am a Senior Scientist for a chemical company and some of my work duties include writing reports and articles; keeping up with trends on new chemical areas to explore; leadership (managing young chemist); consumer demands on new product developments; and transforming everyday essentials to products people can both eat or use on our skin and hair (two key areas related to the business, for example).

Funny thing is, maybe that love of writing came indirectly because I had to write a thesis and dissertation during graduate school, but I now know I can do it. The last part of my graduate school journey taught me a lot about how I write, my format, and the thinking that goes into the process. Everyone has their own style and mine is a bit like a story with relation to my heart. *What does that mean, Donovan?* I write based on feeling and the effects of the topic (or whatever the case may be) on me, this allows me to connect my mind to the words and it produces a passage. I used a similar strategy with my dissertation, and I managed to get five chapters (I later turned three out of the five chapters into scientific publications) and over 150 pages (wipes head right now….).

This book is no different. It will, however, be my first piece of art. I live a periodic lifestyle for the most part, you can blame it on me being a scientist or a Virgo (yes, I was born in September). Just like this book, I value key steps such as: 1) identifying your current state of mind, 2) using the scientific method (or some other process) to overcome your problem, and 3) moving on to the next level. This may seem very generic and elementary, but it is not. Thus far, it has worked for me. Ask me in the next 40 years if I am still employing this strategy...I think I will say "yes". Nevertheless, it can be very hard for me at times, depending on the situation and, of course, the person or people involved. I believe many of us (this includes me) go through life storms, but instead of moving beyond the storm, we stay there for many reasons such as:

- not knowing that we are in a battle
- scared of what the next step would be
- the chaos is okay since it involves love-ones, family, and close friends
- no strategy for moving on
- prior experience of generational hurt being accepted
- fear

These are just a few common examples ... the list can go on for days. By using examples of some of my life storms and roadblocks I faced and presenting them in a poetic format, I hope this book helps you to recognize and overcome the challenges that you may experience. Naturally, since I love science, this book will suggest how to use the Scientific Method (S.M.) (an idea that all of us was taught back in the day) as a tool to help you when you are going through your own storm and to help guide your thought process for overcoming any situation. When I first learned about the S.M., I used it a lot because it helped me to look at the problem/situation from a very focused lens. The big kicker, it provided me with insight on how to move forward and birthed the nuggets I used to fuel my explosion from one level to the next. Points of pride is a phrase I started using in my first research presentation at Georgia Southern University (where I completed my bachelor's degree) and a person from the audience asked me what it meant. I remember replying, "It is where I want you to stop and think". I am using it in this book because the feeling is the same! They will be highlighted throughout the text to allow you to pause and focus your reading.

> **Point of Pride #1:** The key to growth is change and mind-renewal. Lacking those items will keep anyone in the same state, which defeats the mindset of new beginnings.

I really believe the key to growth is change and mind-renewal. This is huge because I have been stuck mentally in so many situations where my actions displayed pure complacency (being in relationships where it is just okay or doing only the minimum required to just pass the class are a few examples). Lacking the capability to renew my mind which is connected to my actions prevented my growth. I had to (and I will probably continue to do so) change so I can yield my elevation because I did not want to reside in the same state of mind, which defeats the mindset of new beginnings. Take it from me and let this book be a guide to your tomorrow!

REAGENT LIST

TO START...

The fundamental purpose of this book is to encourage the reader to be strong in all circumstances. Strength is gained by exercising and/ or practicing how to be strong. Consider athletes that start off as a beginner and later become experts or coaches. Also, it is a trait that comes when confidence is present, and fear is removed. The hard part is the latter, removing fear. Fear is the mind-killer. However, courage combats it, and it is a "cousin" of strength in as much as it speaks to the ability of doing something. Being strong does not mean that the individual must be loud, hardcore, mean, or stubborn to their ways. No, it represents that the person must "stand tall" against the opponent (such as: another person, a situation, job challenge, overcoming a health scare, recovery, loss of a family member or friend, financial instability, and etc.). How it shows is different for every person. That is key, because at times, we compare our strengths to others. There may be someone in an argument that handles conflict with silence versus another individual who uses colorful, decorated, or big words when in a disagreement. The take-home message about the last example is your strength is defined by you only!

Point of Pride #2: your strength is defined by only you!

Another point of this book is to drive you to find that inner fire and elevate yourself beyond your current circumstance. I wrote this during a time when my mind was exposed to hurt, searching for avenues to escape trouble, family was not close to me as expected, friendship dynamics were not desired, perceptions of reality were different than what the output was, life was throwing major hurdles at me all at once, and my wish for a cure to the madness was to simply write.

My love for S.T.E.M. (Science, Technology, Engineering, and Mathematics), with a focus on Science, led me to think about the scientific method and how it could be applied to life. With the scientific method, there is always a start and finish, cause and effect, action and reaction, and a problem and solution. The best way to overcome any situation and face a roadblock is to have a strategy, a periodic process. I use it often! From the basics of its origin, the scientific method has steps that are key to strategize through problems:

1. Make an observation or identification.
2. Ask a question.
3. Form a hypothesis, or testable explanation.
4. Make a prediction based on the hypothesis.
5. Test the prediction/ Data collection
6. Iterate: use the results to make new hypotheses or predictions.
7. Summarize

Using the steps mentioned above (in a similar fashion that suits your taste) will help one to navigate and possibly come through the storm better than you entered it. The first part, which is the most important step, helps one to identify what is the problem. Many times, we as humans are blinded by outside factors such as, bias, love, family, money, friendship, history, and being content, just to name a few. Asking a question sets the individual up to clarify the observation phase. This will then lead you to form an assumption based off what you identified. That will need to go through various tests (this phase can be the longest) and proving. This stage can be interesting because it can present different perspectives that may be unknown or uncomfortable to address. Nevertheless, it is key because going through the testing will enable you to focus on the data. Now, you have all the information and facts that you need, and it will be your time to summarize your scientific method. The results should lead to your winning solution: strength over your circumstance!

> **Point of Pride# 3:** ....going through the testing will enable you to focus on the data.

Placing everything together, 1) being strong, 2) using a strategy will bring defeat to any roadblock 3) and changing your mind to move on will elevate you to your "next". The ideal case is possessing all at once, a masterplan for success. Life does not always give you every tool. At times, we will have one component and not the other which slows down the process of getting through the darkness. That can, and will, be okay. The reason is, sometimes strength or being strong forms under pressure, like a diamond. The process yields a strong product, it does not start with one. It is the process that creates the strength.

The scientific method is an old concept taught in grade school that has proven to be an effective tool in scientific exploration and it can also be applied to daily life. You can put the scientific method to work for you to get you through your hurt, build or increase your resilience, and overcome your (or any) circumstance.

PART 1

What Are My situations?

The first part of this book will be a collection of essays that convey situations, thoughts, and approaches that illustrate how to overcome the struggles you may be facing. Some are personal and others are generic.

When the Roadblock Re-Directs You

When a roadblock has re-directed you, what happens next? How does it feel to be re-directed? Is it a roadblock or merely a detour? These are just a few questions that come across my mind regarding roadblocks. The idea of a roadblock means that a barrier exists between you and your destination. This implies that your journey has stopped or slowed down.

When the signs say to go another way......

A road block can be many things such as, the police stopping someone at a rest stop, a student failing a class, a car accident when someone is in route to their destination, the loss of an ID card while on tour, and the list goes on. To be clear, it is the median between your start and finish. The interesting idea behind the middle component in a journey is the fact that your destination is not erased, it is only modified. Looking at one of the examples above, a car accident is a horrible situation. Hurt, pain, financial hits, and suffering are ingredients that could arise from such an event. No one leaves their initial destination and say, "I want to get into a car accident." However, what if the building/school/or home that you were traveling to went up in flames after your car accident? The destination no longer exists, which would mean your whole journey would have been for nothing. I am sure that most people would prefer to not get into an accident, because it means the end destination is still there … it just may take a bit longer to reach it. Therefore, the car accident was merely a road-block that forced one to find an alternate route to the destination.

In the same way, some situations may attack us as roadblocks, but they are compass tools that send us into another route. The GPS is the perfect example of a "re-directing" device; however, it does not warn of impending road blocks. This is key because avoiding road blocks help us avoid harsher hurts, bruises, and pains. But not many people can identify a road block until it is upon them. Even then, we view it in a very situational perspective: a nuisance, headache, and unwanted annoyance. However, when you have faith and hope in God, you realize that the road block was installed by His will. Is the roadblock really re-routing you to your blessing? **When you pray for protection, a barrier that appears in your path may, in fact, be guiding you to another highway to travel … the ultimate GPS system.** *Let that sink in before moving on to the next paragraph.*

The next time a roadblock has redirected you, consider all the components involved. Think about whether you should *stop* or *slow down*, figure what could be learned at that given time, reconsider your destination, and jump back into motion. **A change in your journey should not deaden your desire; it should only add energy to modify the process.**

How Strong Are You?

One of my biggest accomplishments was achieving my Ph.D. in Organic Chemistry from the University of Florida. The day I walked across the stage, I knew it was a dream come true simply because I destroyed a stigma: "Black men do not attain Ph.D.s…..particularly, not in Chemistry/Science fields." I come from a family that values education and many of my relatives are educated, from bachelor's degrees to doctorates. However, in my generation, I was the first to obtain the highest degree and it was in a scientific field. This was a major accomplishment.

Every success story has a road less traveled: *the struggle.* While I was an undergraduate, my mind was set on attending graduate school in a S.T.E.M. field after I completed three scientific internships in and out of the country: Georgia Institute of Technology (Atlanta, Georgia); Graz Institute of Technology (Graz, Austria); and University of Florida (Gainesville, Florida). I loved doing research because it helped me to discover ideas, contribute to science, and challenge my way of thinking. Also, I researched at my home institution which was Georgia Southern University (Statesboro, Georgia). The above experiences became very essential to my pursuit towards my graduate education because it catered to one of the entrance requirements: RESEARCH. The other aspects graduate schools looked for on an aspirant's application were GRE score, letters of recommendation (LOR), and GPA. The weight on the order just mentioned are heavy > medium > light. The research component fit between GRE score and LOR. I was strong in every requirement bracket except for the GRE score. They were not high enough. Most schools wanted a score of above 1200 (on a scale of 1600) and mine was lower than that. But I never lost hope.

I applied to ten schools and was accepted by three of them. I choose the University of Florida because it was a big-name school, had a lot of opportunities of research, is close to my hometown of Savannah, Georgia, and it had a ranked chemistry program in the world (#36 at the time). Despite their decision to accept me, they placed me on academic probation for the first semester because my GRE score was lower than their requirement. This meant I had to over-perform in my course work to obtain a GPA of 3.6 and above in order to stay in the program. This was my first trial. This was *pressure* because the classes were hard, but I was not leaving without a fight. I worked hard and pushed through, and in the end, I completed my first semester with a 3.7. I wiped my forehead as a sign of relief. The feeling of conquering those classes was beyond grateful.

The next struggle presented itself when I made a B- in one of my courses during my 4th semester (2nd year). The lowest grade a graduate student can make in any graduate school program is a B. My research advisor (RA) had to write a recommendation letter to keep me in the program. Some may say, that should be easy. Well, it was not because he had little to go from. I selected him as my RA at the beginning of my 3rd semester and I performed very little research in his group at the time. He wrote the letter anyway and held several meetings with the Deans of the College of Liberal Arts and Sciences (CLAS) to keep me in the program because he said, "his fighting potential to be great in the scientific field far outweighs one course to characterize his academic integrity."

> **Point of Pride #4:** ... "his fighting potential to be great in the scientific field far outweighs one course to characterize his academic integrity."

With the support of my RA, I knew I was in route towards graduation. However, each graduate student had to obtain 4 points (1 full point or half point based from the score set by the professor giving the cumulative written examination) for 9 subject based chemistry exams during the 2nd and 3rd year of the program. To clarify, Professor X can give an exam and set his full point to be anything above 85% and half point to be anything above 65%. Those grade percentages vary by professor, some are more lenient than others. I was doing very well on the first few exams; I made a few full points. The intensity increased, and the professors started giving harder exams and I failed a few (obtained no points). It came to exam number 9, the last one, and my overall score was 3.5 so I was scared. Fear showed itself and was very strong in my face. At this point, I am sure I thought about quitting, giving up, or making an alternative life plan. Having faith and tapping into my strength toolbox was very slow. Before taking it, I prayed very hard, studied for hours daily, held several practice sessions with other students, and did EVERTHING chemistry. I found some fight in me and I was determined and passionate. **The rule is, if a student does not make 4.0 points on the cumulative examinations, he/she will have to accept a master's degree and reapply to the Ph.D. program.**

In my opinion, it was a fancy way of kicking a student out; *I was not going out like that. The lion (my favorite animal) in me became stronger and stronger! My thoughts were equivalent to a lion's roar.*

Image of a lion in its natural state of roaring loudly.

At times, I would go sit on the stairs of the church I attended just to pray and ask God to speak to me. Some nights, I felt I heard His voice. I spoke to my friends about my situation and many of them gave encouraging words to get me over the hump. My thoughts before the day of the test were:

Every semester since the beginning, I had to fight to stay in this program. Why did this journey seem so hard and less exciting? Am I cut out for this type of accomplishment or task? If I conquered the struggles from the past, I could overcome this one. Do I have that much strength and why must I show it just to make it to another struggle? What If I do not past this exam, what is next for me? What if I *do, what will the next struggle be? This was a major pill to swallow because my level of academic success was based on **one exam**. I MUST WIN!*

That last thought gave me the gasoline to drive my car over the winning line. I walked into the exam and made a ½ point which gave me the required 4.0 points for the cumulative examinations. At this point in my graduate career, when I asked myself, "How strong are you?", I replied, "Strong enough to win the battles that I am faced with." Gaining that mentality was growth because I never had it before, and it helped in later struggles. To add, it carried me throughout the rest of my Ph.D. journey; I never viewed anything as "hard." I looked at tasks as achievable and I aimed to accomplish everything I was presented with. After that, I obtained four literature publications, started focusing on my research, traveled to give presentations at many conferences and schools, spent time in Dresden, Germany as a Visiting Scientist at the Polymer Research Institute of Dresden, mentored an exchange student from Japan, graduated with my Ph.D. in Organic Chemistry, and acquired a career at an industrial Chemical Company (AkzoNobel).

Being In a Storm Without an Exit

What is a storm? How does it feel to be in the eye of a hurricane or in the middle of a thunderstorm? What happens if you're in a continual snowstorm? With those questions in mind, consider the exit or end nowhere in sight. Typically, when people walk into a room, situation, house, car, building, etc., the expectation is to walk back out, or exit.

> **Point of Pride #5:** During a storm is when we really apply concepts such as: how to learn, what to think, how to feel, and what to do in efforts to be strong.

Yes, in most cases, the news can anticipate or predict a storm. However, life is not always that predictable. If it were, everyone would be able to avoid storms. When we enter them, fear kicks in and the struggle causes bones to break. During a storm is when we really apply concepts such as: how to learn, what to think, how to feel, and what to do in efforts to be strong.

I faced a situation where I initially saw no exit during one of my storms. When I stayed in Graz, Austria, I got very sick in my apartment. Days before the major event, I felt slight pains in my chest, but I ignored it because I thought Tylenol could cure it. I was wrong. I woke up one morning in major pain. Blood was coming from my nose and I could not move, the left side of my chest was in major pain. At the time, I did not have a roommate, so I had no one to help me. My thoughts of how to mitigate the situation were diluted because my pain escalated. But I knew I needed someone to take me to the hospital. Therefore, I crawled out of my bed to my computer, so I could skype a friend that lived in the same apartment complex. He came to help rush me to the emergency room (ER) and the storm became stronger.

The doctors at the hospital in Austria did not speak English and, as a result, they could not identify my sickness. This was scary because I spent two nights in the ER with no success. Various blood tests and scans were completed, and it led to no conclusions. Let me add, none of my family members stayed in Austria and my friends were from school (so I felt alone during this struggle). They transported me to another hospital with more specialized doctors. For two weeks after I arrived there, they went through more testing to identify what was wrong and how to treat me. During that time, they contacted my parents who were in the U.S. It was discovered that I had bronchitis and pneumonia at the same time. According to the doctors, this was a horrible combination. It took three weeks for me to heal back to normal and then I was transported back home.

During that storm mentioned above, I did not see an exit and I was in pain, clueless, and distant/lonely. Because of the doctors' initial inability to diagnose why I was sick; the darkness became darker. It made me feel like I acquired a disease (and they refer to sickness as "disease" in Austria so that did not help my thinking…) or major infection. How did I get through that situation? I found books to read, learned German, and I spoke with other patients on many topics. Every day, I wrote how I wanted to feel in efforts to coerce my mind to that state. Also, I took walks around the hospital to change my setting. Ultimately, I MADE THE EXIT.

Point of Pride #6: Where is your exit?

My decision was to not allow the pain to win and to fight back by doing those things I mentioned above. The exit was created in my mind and my brain mentally left the storm. There is a stopping point to every snowstorm, thunderstorm, and hurricane and it indicates the ending of such a disaster. Life is similar, yet we have more autonomy over *our* storms by making the decision to end them. Where does the strength come from to make such a decision? It comes from the power gained during the *recovery*.

The Recovery

According to the various dictionary sources (Merriam-Webster, dictionary.com, and others), the word *recovery* means to "get back" or "return to a normal state." It can be implied that a *loss* took place or a *down period* which will eventually lead to a "rebuild." Indeed, this is true in many aspects of life: biological, medical, social, financial, mental, personal, etc. However, why is the recovery stage so important during a storm?

Considering it from a medical perspective, this stage represents a period of change in which individuals improve their bodies and wellness and attempt to reach a higher potential than when they were prior to being sick. Financially, people may develop plans to save money, investigate ways to increase investments, or spend less to refine their finances. Consider our skin. Our skin can biologically recover itself if a bruise or cut happens. Mental recovery is like the above examples; people begin to figure out ways of improvement, think of how to change their situation, investigate how to be happy again, repair, and restore the mind and heart. All the cases have one underlying theme in common: hope emerges and there are many pathways. So, there is no one route to recovery. What does it mean to have hope? Well, it depends on who is being asked but generally, it is the expectation of a positive result. It is a very optimistic feeling. Another description of hope is like expecting a promotion after you have launched a successful initiative in your company which yielded a major financial return. When cancer cannot be found in a cancerous cell, when weight loss occurs, or when your hunger was addressed by a scrumptious steak ... these are signs of the hope feeling. To clarify, it is like a happy mental "high."

> **Point of Pride #7:** Hope is like a happy mental "high." One factor to comprehend is that recovery deals with hope that forces to change.

When hope is present, there is a mental shift which pushes the individual from one stage to another (a sad to a happy stage; a depressed or defeated to a conquering stage). That change is the crucial part of the recovery because it is a step change on a ladder or the elevation from one level to the next. One factor to comprehend is that recovery deals with *hope that forces change*.

Understanding this will keep you strong during a down period or never allow comfort to sit in during the *storm*. Once complacency kicks in, recovery never begins, and a bed is made in the "dark period." Actively recovering involves key steps mentioned below:

1. Identify the current state of mind you are in -- sad, depressed, or etc.
2. Face the dynamic of what it entails
3. Realize there is a way out
4. Write down a strategy and a blueprint that will lead you to that *change*
5. Create an action plan and hold yourself accountable
6. Understand the small milestones during the process as a way for encouragement
7. Complete the action plan and review the learnings
8. Tell yourself that you recovered the struggle and notice the difference!
9. Shout that you have recovered

Fighting a Battle Un-Equipped

In a battle, there are two types of people: winner and loser. Or, they can be described as someone who is ready for battle versus someone who is not. However, just because you are prepared for the battle, does not necessarily mean you will be victorious. What or who ultimately determines the victor? The answer is not one-worded ... there are layers to this question. Nevertheless, we know that drive and motivation results in victory. There are countless examples of "un-equipped" people (for example, David versus Goliath in the Bible) or underdogs who unexpectedly won a battle. The inspiration behind this essay is not focused on winners and losers. Rather, it is focused on being "un-equipped."

Being unprepared and not ready are state of minds that will only lead to subordinate end results. The reason is simple, the **effort must match the destination**. Stop and think about this point, it is key! Numerous situations exist that will un-equip someone such as: death in the family (kills motivation to move forward when experienced a lost); failing a test (burns self-esteem in your course work); infidelity in marriage (ruins trust); being fired from your job (makes one feel hopeless). Those are just a few examples. It is standard to shut down or just give up in these situations. It can be a domino effect in which one situation affects another, furthering the process of taking away your equipment. I do believe that the situations of life prepare us for our next steps and some of them are out of our control (a topic for another essay). When any of those circumstances happen, does time stop or does life hit the pause button? The answer is NO. The fight or daily battles continue to propagate on! Just to be clear, our day-to-day (work, family, bills, goals, children, spouse, etc.) is representation of the fight.

Therefore, one must not continue to be un-equipped during the battle. We are all human so catching your breath during your storm is acceptable, but do not stop moving. There is effort in your state of defeat or unreadiness. It is coined as "drive." During the colder months, cars are not ready to move at the start of the day. However, once started, that horsepower kicks in, energy is being generated, the oil is pumping, the car moves, and performs according to the driver. We are no different than cars. We can allow "our horsepower" to be our minds encouraging ourselves, "the energy" is our hearts pumping harder based on our motivation to navigate through the storm, and the oil is the blood that flows within us despite whether we are winning or losing! This only means that our mental state of being unequipped transitions to "ready" during battle based on our effort.

Fighting with the Right Weapons

The thought or perception of war and/or battle will always be an ongoing event. Life has so many cases where it exists such as in the Bible, country versus country; family members against each other; you against you; school rivalries; competing companies or products; and the list goes on. In every battle, there are two main components: winner and loser. It may be hard to digest that an event that is played out in daily activities since the beginning of time to the death of it contains only those two parts. However, please understand the significance of each and it will help you decide which you will become.

There are many examples of winners and, of course, this is the desired route. Consider the story of David versus Goliath. This was interesting because Goliath was a warrior and the champion of Philistines. He was trained to fight and win. Also, he was a huge,

19

intimidating man. According to the Bible, Goliath would challenge the Israelites twice a day for a combat and he stressed that he only wanted their champion. As the story unfolds, young David accepts the challenge and approaches his adversary with a staff and five stones. The result is well-known ... David defeats him with one shot.

Another interesting history lesson was the battle of New England Patriots versus the New York Giants in the 2008 Super Bowl. Throughout the season leading up to the Super Bowl, the Patriots were undefeated with a 19-0 record and their quarterback Tom Brady was the "poster child for the greatest of all times." Nevertheless, he won the MVP award and they were determined to make history, leaving a season with no losses by winning the Super Bowl. Their opponent, the Giants, had energy, determination, and something to prove to the world. Leading up to the championship game, the Giants slowly clinched their way into the main event by defeating the teams in their path despite an okay season with their quarterback Eli Manning. This team was the underdog. During the Super Bowl, the game was tough, close, and the Giants scored 14 points (two touchdowns and 1-point safety kicks) during the final quarter to lead with a score of 17-14 with just minutes before the game's conclusion. They still had drive and they used it to prevent Brady from completing passes. When the Giants won the game, many football fans were left scratching their heads and wondering how the best team with the best quarterback lost.

The answer to that was that the Giants fought with the right weapons: *courage and huge foresight.* When an opponent or a person has courage, it provides ammunition to conquer anything. Typically, both the winners and loser in a battle possess some ounce of courage. Let's focus on "huge foresight" which exemplifies big future. Most winners that were considered underdogs did not focus on their opponent, they focused beyond their opponent, into the *big future*. For example, if David would have focused on Goliath or the Giants focused on the Patriots, both would have resulted in losses due to what they perceived as an insurmountable opponent. Therefore, giving attention to the **defeat** of a warrior and a **win** in the Super Bowl gave light to the dark battle.

In life, people should focus not on their situation, but the outcome they desire. Possessing a mentality such as this leads to a winning thought which carries over to a successful product or result. Winners never think about losing; they use one major defeat mechanism: *winner's mentality*.

"A lion does not concern itself with the opinions of sheep."

Famous expression that was quoted by Tywin Lannister in the "Game of Thrones"

The lion has many admirable characteristics, including being a leader, dominant, king-like, strong, powerful, fearless, big, loud, courageous, royal, and authoritative. When one visits a zoo, the lions are one of the biggest attractions there. Because of their size, strength, and power, lions usually require more separation from humans (bigger cages and barricades separating them from human contact, excluding the zoo's staff). They can be the most dangerous animal in some cases. When they roar, it is felt from afar and it can be intimidating (they produce loud roars without exerting much pressure on their lungs). The roar can be heard close to five miles away. Other known facts about them are that their heels do not touch when they walk, their night vision is much more sensitive than humans, and they can go without drinking water for days. Simply stated, they are just different. They are superior!

With those things in mind, how does the image of a lion play out in real life? That question is situational, and it depends on a few factors, such as self-awareness and motivation. This list can be exhausted, but it is limited to drive home a specific point. In respect to a person, knowing your self-worth and capabilities are key variables of understanding self-awareness. A person's weaknesses (we all have them) and strengths should be apparent to the individual and not withheld in secret. This will allow continuous improvement and "you" being the measuring stick. To expound on this note regarding today's time, social media, the news, and other technological outlets encourages false impressions of reality. Billionaires, big businesses, two-parent household with children, beach or large houses, nice neighborhoods with well paved streets, nice (sporty and/or luxury) cars, trendy style, healthy athletic bodies, and much more are becoming the standards to achieve. Those are linked with the individuals that own (or rent in some to most cases) those items. They become very nice pictures but not totally real.

What is not being shown in the pictures mentioned above are the process from start to finish: how that millionaire became one; the cars or no transportation the person had before the sporty ride; how small the business was before it took off to yield big returns; and the chaos that exist within the two-parent household. This is just a few examples. A suggestion, if more people understood the before and after, it may direct people to take a structured methodology to achieve items they desire (this may also link itself to the capability of the person). Therefore, when those nice-have images become the "standard," it is a plastic approach to someone's version of success. To combat that, I try to convey my measuring stick to be me from yesterday and what I want to accomplish, which is aligned with my passionate tokens. Those are the impact factors I want to employ within science, the black community, and the tie between education and industry. If allowing yourself to become the measurable, self-worth and self-awareness will only become more defined and the standard will become your growth.

> **Point of Pride #8:** Motivation is slightly related to your self-worth because it has correlations to what a person thinks they are capable of and can achieve.

Motivation is related to your self-worth because it has correlation to what a person thinks they are capable of and can achieve. As continuous growth occurs within a person, it begins to affect their financial status, how they manage their relationships (at work, social, and family), and things they aspire to obtain and accomplish. So, the drive behind the motivation will be truly focused on your happiness, your impact and not tied to anyone or anything else.

Going back to the lion, let's see how this image plays out in life. Just like the lion, if a person has a "roar" that can exceed (for miles) other animal's alarm system, walk differently, doesn't require the same essentials as others, and is very commanding; they will not compete with or compare themselves to others. They will know that they are different and realizing this fact separates them from the crowd. To every lion there are numerous sheep. Sheep are smaller, timid, and less aggressive than lions. In fact, the differences between lions and sheep are numerous. The person's approach and swag to life (whether it is educational attainment, dating, or financial security) may be based off their values and goals. This is key when it is being discussed in relation to your self-worth and motivation. Value is engrained in who you are; it is your self-awareness which leads to your motivation and your continuous growth. The reasons above are a collective few of why lions do not worry about the opinions of sheep. The sheep represent the masses…the average person. Lions are not average… they are just different!

Success Is Defined by Failure, Not Victories.

What is a victory? This can be defined very differently depending on who you ask and the person's state of mind. Generally, a victory is when an action has been achieved, a barrier knocked down, an accomplishment is reached, or a tangible reward is given because of doing something spectacular. According to dictionary.com, one of the definitions of victory is "a success or superior position achieved against any opponent, opposition, difficulty." One of my ongoing thoughts has always been, why does society mostly correlate success with victory? I would argue that it is only a by-product of it and success should be more aligned with failure. I know it sounds weird because one represents a positive and the other a negative. Nevertheless, in a science world, when the different states of matter meet, it leads to a neutral outcome, so they attract.

> **Point of Pride #9:** One of my ongoing thoughts has always been, why does society mostly correlate success with victory?

Looking at success, dictionary.com defines it "as the favorable or prosperous termination of attempts or endeavors; the accomplishment of one's goals." This describes an interesting narrative especially when considering "prosperous termination of attempts or endeavors" which convey failure or lack of a victory. When we as humans face losing a battle, not achieving a milestone, or something similar, we define it as failure. Then, when the situation turns itself around, we typically jump to the word victory. However, it is often the response to our failures and our determination to learn from them and move past them that leads us to victory. My question is why not consider success when failure presents itself?

Let's ponder a general example of a student who submitted a remarkable (the student thought it was perfect.) paper (5-7 pages in length) which took him/her a few weeks to complete. The grade the student received was a D. To the student, it feels like a failed assignment; technically, they did due to every letter grade holding some numerical value. On the flip side of the situation, success did present itself, even if it was not realized at that moment. The student's takeaways from the incident included:

- feedback was given by the professor to explain why the letter grade was received
- remarks were included with explanations of what was written wrong (grammar, mechanical, and possibly diction errors)
- *an opportunity to do it again (even if it was not for the same class or assignment)*

The last bullet point holds the most weight and it is the true definition of success because it is taking the failures (the remarks and feedback) to apply it as potential success tokens. This is key and why I believe the two words should be more related. For example, on the next assignment or writing opportunity, the student took the feedback from the previous assignment and was able to apply them to the new paper, which earned a much higher grade. Failure presents challenges to our existing mindset. It forces us to evaluate our current process and find a new way of thinking, after all, we cannot expect novel outcomes if our process is unchanged. Failure helps us understand our strengths, weaknesses, and limitations. All of these are vital if you want to be successful on a next writing assignment, or whatever your next task is. Failure is the teaching bridge to success. Success should be defined by our ability to learn from failure, and not by our ability to achieve victory. On the bridge, the learning capability is so wide, the person becomes more knowledgeable about the situation and the process should not be ignored. Therefore, next time your faced with failure, consider it a success due to the knowledge you will gain towards your upcoming victory.

Family Matters

Family is of high importance to almost everyone. Family is the nucleus of many generations, cultures, societies, entities, corporations, and organizations. It means a unit, togetherness, and a group of people. The word "family" will be used in a general sense, excluding the use of nuclear and extended families. Several TV shows and movies, such as *Family Matters*, *Black-ish*, *This Is Us*, *Mike and Molly*, and *The Incredibles* describe various components of what family is about. These fictional and non-fictional stories give the public a general idea that "family" means blood-line, but it is also much more than that. These movies and TV shows depict every family member live and grow up together; two-parent household with grandparents; the close relation-ships of sibling groups; and staying within the family/ biological circle to host/participate in holiday/ and some non-holiday traditions. This is a generalization and not entirely factual; however, it perpetuates the idea that family is bound by genetics *only*. I want to challenge that thought because **family is made up of humans (*the first race and the equality amongst us all according to Dr. Martin Luther King Jr.*) first!**

This is to not discredit any culture, tribe, and family that have built in closeness within their framework. That is a great thing, an ideal scenario. However, family does not only refer to bloodline or people that are related to a person biologically. Some attributes of being in a family or a part of one are listed below:

- Understanding heritage and culture
- Meeting and building bonds with relatives
- Support, love, nurturing, and passing down norms and values
- Being a member of a collective group of people
- Holiday traditions and celebrations

The items listed above are great and they add to the development of every individual (from infant to adulthood). With that, expectation is created, and everyone anticipates their family members to contribute to the group in those fashions. This is the ultimate mistake. The main question is, why have we limited some of those traits only to our bloodline? Non-family members can sometimes offer the same (and more in some cases, depending on your direct situation) benefits. Speaking directly to the mistake of creating family expectations, when someone does not hold up their end of the deal (even if they were never made aware of it), chaos and turmoil begins. This is a part of life, but it will or can impact the individual differently since most people create standards of family members based on some of the attributes listed above. With standards, brings levels. Simply stated or an example of this phenomenon, you may make an excuse about a family member's action but cut someone off that is a non-family member for doing the same action. What is up with that?

> **Point of Pride #10:** With standards, brings levels! Let this sink in because it is an action that is done by us all without thought, we just do it in some cases.

My thoughts are to accept who your family is generally, and not keep it specific to your bloodline. Expectations and standards will always generate themselves but removing the levels will, or may, allow all of us to look at humans as family members and family members as humans. Some of my closest friends are considered family and some of my biological members are considered friends/associates. However, I do have biological relatives that I consider family. To place emphasis on my familial make-up, it consists of mother, brothers, sisters, nieces, cousins, grandparents, close friends, god- parents (the other family that has been very involved in my life since growing up; and parents that took me in while I traveled the world during school and etc.). To name a few bad apples, some of my cousins on my father side disowned me and/or displayed jealous tendencies while I was growing up; and my father left my immediate family and decided that my mother should raise boys on her own (we all turned out pretty awesome so I am appreciative of his action, to be honest…. but that's another topic). Nevertheless, I look at them as humans first, so when non-family members show similar actions, my responses to their behaviors are equal. On the contrary, when non-relatives show love, support, and admiration towards me in any way (providing praise, calling to check on me, ensuring that I am not in need, and other key examples), I consider them family because it means to me **bonds being built, not genetics *only*.** This would be like some of my bloodline family that continue to show love since my birth.

Out of Comfort Is Where Resilience Is Built

Resilience can come in many forms such as recovering from a hardship, a force being applied to a spring and it is bouncing back to its original state, or the incorporation of a chemical entity into a final product which goes against an external force disrupting the primary function. With all of that said, resilience is the manufacturing of strength and this is done out of our comfort zones. Places where we feel okay, complacent, satisfied, and doable are all signs of being in our comfort zones. We live our daily lives in our comfort zone. It is the job we go to everyday for 15+ years doing the same work, the organization we have been a part of that has not grown or caused a change within us but we like the people, or the relationship which simply "works" (not for the better or it cannot get any worse but your content with where it is at the moment).

How do we grow if we never eat? How will we succeed or excel if we don't apply? How do we elevate ourselves if we continue to look straight out and not up? Those are just a few questions I ponder about when examining where I am at versus where I want to go. Another one to consider is "how do we establish that we are comfortable?" This is key (and it should be treated case by case to be frank) because to change something, you must **identify** the current state. Note: the main word to pay attention to is "identify." Before moving on, go look in a mirror, remove all distractions (so leave your phone, lock the kids out and ignore the spouse for 2 minutes).

Now, consider 2 ways to identify that you are in your comfort zone:

1. Ask yourself how your current situation affects your next steps. *This will help you determine if you are thinking about change and what is next.*
2. Simply ask yourself if you are being challenged and in what way. *This may help you determine if the challenge for growth exist for your current state of mind or if it is nonexistent (then why is it absent).*

After you realized if you are in the comfort zone, then put a **plan** in motion to change the narrative. The plan can be as fundamental as asking a series of questions, such as "what am I doing now?," "what do I want to do within the next six months or year?," and "how can

I make this work to shift me from where I am at to where I want to be?" *This is where resilience is built.* Jumping out is easy but you will experience pressure -- the struggles of learning a new job; headache of joining a new company where you will learn new people, culture, and environment; uncertainty of opening a new business in a new market; not knowing anyone in a new city; going on a second or third date with a guy/girl you have crushed on for some time; and the list goes on. As a result, the pressure molds you to your next level by you becoming a master at the new job; climbing the ladder at the new company thanks to a strong work ethic and new mindset; and your company exploding in the market because consumers like innovative solutions/companies. Without the process, resilience is removed, but with it is where the next level is achieved or at least attempted!

PART 2

How Can I Use the Scientific Method?

This section will deal with the scientific method approach to address obtaining your victory through a storm, but with a strategy! But first, let's define what the scientific method is. View the picture below. There are many variations of this model, but in general it reads as follows:

Generic picture of the Scientific Method (S.M.)

This method is an important one to me because it is easy and straightforward. It has been widely used for many decades and it is systematic. The steps within each phase are the support one would need to go to the next phase. Like the picture suggest above, there are about five specific steps in the S.M. If you think about it, why not relate it to your life and getting through a storm, solving a problem, advancing your current mindset, reaching a decision, and countless other scenarios where it can be applied. This part will focus on the application of it in you! Read on!

What Is the Problem?

Has anyone ever asked you, "What is the problem?" How did you answer the question? Or, have you gone through an issue or was affected by your situation where you had to ask yourself that same question? Thinking of the *what* is starts to change the narrative. Science is the field where we assess problems by providing solutions via the scientific method, but the problem needs to be identified (whether it is in response to or an improvement of your situation). This can be done in countless ways. For example, the need to replace plastics with biodegradable alternatives to affect greenhouse gas emissions; the need for green hydrogen to aid in the conversion of renewables to hydrogen back to electricity; or to chemically combat the growing widespread of illnesses like cancer and sickle cell anemia. Being practical and applying the scientific method to a normal human, how do we answer that question or identify a problem?

In terms of combating a situation (an easier method), one would simply be affected, abused, or attacked which would lead to a retaliation response. In most cases, this decision-making period for this type of response can be quick with very little thought about the outcome, which could affect your *design of experiments strategy* (next section). For example, if some random person hits you in the face on the subway, you want to defend yourself by either hitting them back or bracing yourself for another possible hit. There is nothing wrong with responding when things don't go your way, but a knee-jerk approach is rather swift, and it involves limited thinking due to result of *reactive* action.

Let's consider the opposition of reactivity and consider proactivity. This is the harder method. Chemistry allows us to have a forward view of problems that will arise and makes us consider how we should attack them by being proactive. In the same sense, this can be applied to us. This is not a suggestion to find a problem to fix. Instead, it is more of a starting point to change the narrative. This is case by case of course. For example, being in a relationship with your partner for five plus years where you both are happy. Do you consider how to take the level of happiness to the next stage and a strategy? Another one can be your current work situation where you have been employed with a company for years (You may be content there because they have given you promotions and a few job title changes), but have you considered changing into a new role within a new division of the company? Or, even taking your talent capability to another organization? In both cases, the answer to "what is the problem?" is addressed by the desire to change or elevate to the next level. However, let us back it up. If we are happy and content, how do we get to the stage to identify the problem?

Getting to that stage is the acceptance of changing the narrative or wanting something new. Time changes every second on the second and the seasons change four times a year. So, when it is understood that change is a proactive answer to that question is when you start the process. Yes, there is thinking involved in this madness, allowing you to consider where you are at and where you want to go (in the simplest terms of course). Relating this to molecule creation, chemists spend countless hours in the lab looking at an existing chemical structure and the question that arises is two-fold: how do we use that compound to make something new, and how can that compound be made differently? This thought comes from the need of being proactive and the desire to tap into what is to come. Therefore, address your "what is the problem" by having a forward lens to change the narrative or exploring the newness behind your situation. There is only one main requirement to enforce this: to think!

Design of Experiments

This section of the book will focus more on solutions since the previous part was based on identification of the situational state of mind. In chemistry, we teach students that a solution is a liquid mixture of major (solvent) and minor (solute) components yielding a new product. The fascinating aspect of *solution chemistry* is its application in all walks of life: daily activities such as making a cup of coffee with milk or crème added (a homogenous mixture), putting together a bucket of mop solution (cleaner + water) to clean the floor, and school setting when the example of water and an acid is combined (dilution method). Outside of chemistry, it can be defined as the solving of a problem and we all practice that art to varying degrees. Both have one major correlation which is the result of a "Design of Experiments."

Process is key to any start and finish because it dictates routes to travel and ones to avoid. Of course, the big question is how to define the process to focus it so it is answered within your **design**. In the chemical world, we start with a problem (like the previous section…) or a hypothesis. Then, we list how to solve that issue by a set of trials (within each trial are the specific reactions/experiments). Data is collected and compared for each trial; at that point, the focus is introduced due to the case with the best results. The analysis is done to address whether the set of experiments provides a solution or come close to one. In an ideal world, the first iteration of data points work, and you have a **solution**.

In most cases, it is never that easy and the process or design is the defining moment to your solution. How do you create your design of experiments and when you have gone back to the drawing board, how is that done? To address the first part, look at your problem bearing no fear of you not obtaining the answer! This is key because any ounce of doubt will affect how you create your design. Once that is done, create a list of what you can do, what you want to do, and what you will do. Out of those three sections, rank and categorize the items that are most likely to be completed by you. The next task is the hardest within the design of experiment: Execute! It is the hardest because it will be filled with both wins and losses. It will introduce both victory and failure and expose weak areas that you may want to avoid. Most importantly, it affects your mind which is the real bridge between your start and finish. However, it is relevant. Going to the second point, during the execution phase which has become circular (meaning you are back at the drawing board a few times), identify relationships of causes and effects. This method will help you to isolate the good from the mediocre and bad experiments. By doing this, you may revisit some reactions or create new ones which may bear your ultimate solution. To make this more practical, the focus on what you have done versus what you need to do becomes clearer. Emphatically, executing is more definitive and you're closer to your result/ or product. Lastly, take the design of experiments which has been modified during the process, redefined, and conclude what the data represents. Appreciate your process because it is where you learn more about yourself, how to attack a problem (pros and cons), and the outcome of the solution.

> **Point of Pride #11:** "Execution" will introduce both victory and failure and expose weak areas that you may want to avoid.

Get After It

*The drive to execute stems from passion; if you remove it, the "car= you"
will not accelerate.* This is part 2 of the design of experiments phase
because it discusses the action of trusting your process. Cross-fit is a
very intense sport since it involves many components such as: cardio,
powerlifting, weightlifting, and gymnastics. A lot of variables go into
the athlete improving over time from joining a CrossFit gym (start)
to leaving the gym to becoming a professional athlete, consultant/
trainer (the next stage or a semi-finishing training point) or opening
his/her own gym. Like going through many iterations or trials of
reactions, *getting after it* is your vehicle! Every time we get into an
automobile, there is a start and finish point, but the route is the most
important. Your desire or passion to get there faster will lead you to
travel a certain route or your focus to sightsee will direct you to take
another route. It is all in the **feeling** which can be either positive

or negative, this is your choice. That pursuit to going through your process or design must be tapped into. Being in the gym, trying a new movement or learning something, the adrenaline causes us athletes to go hard and keep at it! Having various coaches at the gym, they will facilitate certain techniques based off their style and preference which should encourage you to scout them all (design) in efforts to get to the next phase. The key here is passion which is like fire and that is where the execution begins and continues. To ignite something relates to elevation, and throughout your design of experiments, one way to overcome preventing it from controlling you (more so you have total autonomy over it), a mindset to *get after it* is what you must adopt!

Is the Problem Supported by My Data or Not?

You have all the data and the question is, does it support your hypothesis or not? Scientists collect the results of experimentation, find trends and relationships, and categorize the items based on supporting versus does not support. Often, the predictions of what the problem was is not accurate. This is a similar strategy that we take in our daily lives: 1) looking at the full story, 2) collecting the evidence (whether it is good or bad) based on an assumption, and 3) place data points of information in categories. If this is not a typical strategy for you, please adopt it. Not to quantify and/or stereotype here, but there are three scenarios:

1. Most of your findings fall under supporting evidence of your hypothesis

2. Most of your findings do not fall under supporting evidence of your hypothesis

3. There is a 50/50 chance of supporting evidence of your hypothesis versus non-supporting evidence of your hypothesis.

Scenarios 1 and 2 are easier to deal with because it tells a story, nonetheless. Case 1 suggest that your data support the potential solution to your problem, Case 2 states that potentially there is no solution and it represents poor data. This may cause you to restart your scientific method again. Breaking this point even further, learning can be done through failure and it can happen even if it did not provide a possible fix to your problem. For example, we learn several ways of how not to do things by failing at them first. This is a golden nugget that we should all realize that failure is success *at learning.*

> **Point of Pride #12:** Failure is success at learning. It is okay to fail because it provides countless experiences that one can share or build upon. In society, we try not to fail and only win. That's an okay mindset. However, I challenge the reader to fail happily because positive attributes and discovery come from just failing: strength building, new roads to avoid, another perspective that was once ignored when starting the journey to solve your problem. Fun fact, Dr. Percy Julian (an American Chemist) had an accident in the Glidden Company laboratory, where he was a Research Director, that led to the development of testosterone and birth control pills. The result of that accident is still being used today!

The last scenario is the hardest, what to do if you are in the middle (you have equal amounts of supporting information and non-supporting information)? Several actions can be done at this moment such as: 1) confirm if you are looking at your problem from the right perspective which eventually affects your design of experiments; 2) identify if the analysis of your trials is all consistent, any variation could lead to varying results; 3) gather a second opinion. To place emphasis, restarting the scientific method is key for this scenario as well. Most scientists work in teams and go through series of solving problems. Therefore, an invention or discovery may take years or decades. Action 3 is an important one because another set of eyes can help guide the investigation in the right direction (*but, the other person must be non-bias, this is important*). This is like counseling and what makes this art so effective is if the person seeking counsel is open to criticism and have thought things through. Whether you are in scenarios 1, 2, or 3, collecting the data to make sense of it in efforts to gain a possible solution is a good continuous learning phase to be in. This will only lead you to properly analyze the data to draw a conclusion.

Communicate Your Results

This is the grand finale of your personal scientific method: *communication of your results*. In school or industry, this is done to a large audience; but the impact is heavy when it is done to you by you! This stage involves a final report of published data, understanding of the problem to the solution, modification of the findings to polish the output, and potential comprehension of next steps or how to avoid the reoccurrence of a similar problem. Can this be applied to real life? Yes, simply keep it real and do not make up your own conclusion, ignoring the real one. An old saying is, "the first step in solving a problem is admitting there is one." Additionally, the second part is "once there is a solution to the problem, accept its reality." The big words to remember are identification, acceptance, and communication. When it is time to report your results, it is vital to understand the essence of each of those components.

In high school science fairs, students get dressed up, put together a poster, practice their elevator speeches answering possible questions, and groom themselves to be interrogated. This behavior is also done within any business or government despite the profession. It should be extended to personal lives and communicating the results will be the change to the situation or answer to the problem. How to communicate your results? Keeping it straightforward will enable attention on the content so some strategies are below:

- Purchase a cheap poster board and jot down the conclusion to the results in order
- Create a power point presentation and allow each slide to represent the specific results of your findings
- Use flashcards or Post-It notes to specify the concluding points
- Use a friend, neighbor, mate, or another person to write down the results of your study (while you present it to them) and allow them to present it back to you

There are several ways this can be done, not to limit it to the proposed suggestions mentioned above. However, whichever strategy is done, reflecting on the final report is key to concluding your last stage of the scientific method. Also, having a tangible item will allow you to revisit this study.

PART 3

What Does Moving on Require?

*Time, patience, and an open mind are
key ingredients to moving on.*

This section will require the most thought and application. This will also be the hardest part because moving on is not an easy task. After identifying any problem and going through the necessary steps to overcome it via the scientific method, the "what's next" phase is a mountain. That's the case because it will require perseverance, endurance, effort, and a changed mindset. Those will bring a sense of newness to your life and situation; also, they will elevate you to the next level. Time and patience are to be mentioned as well since they are key supplements to the moving on process. Overcoming an addiction, losing a family member, or removing toxic people from your life are not easy circumstances to overcome. This is especially true when you are dealing with family members, love ones, or a spouse. Within each case just mentioned, the problem was identified, the scientific method was used to provide a solution to it, and now you are at the "next steps" stage. One big question, how do I move on from my comfort zone and/or desires that was hindering me or was my anchor?

Perseverance:

What happens when you want to complete a task but lack energy? What would a person do if they are sick in a rehabilitation center aiming to get better and they are tired of the slow progress? How do people manage to push through their negative inner thoughts when it is pressed against total opposition? The answer to each of those scenarios is the use of perseverance! I would describe it as the energy used by an individual pushing a car with no gas through the snow up a ramp. Just imagine, how hard that could be depending on how thick the snow is and how steep the ramp is. But with perseverance, the task can get done. Consider the experience of director Steven Spielberg. During his academic years while he pursued a degree from University of Southern California School of Theater, Film, and Television, Spielberg got rejection letter after rejection letter on his movie ideas. He also spent time at California State University, however, he never finished his degree there and was rejected from those institutions. He began directing anyway, without a degree, and he found success despite his early failings. He never gave up and his strength to become a movie director is like the individual pushing the car through snow up a ramp. His persistence led to his success.

Energy is strength unused and un-noticed. The latter part is interesting because one would think if we noticed the power we possess, we would never fail. Am I correct? Nevertheless, when that strength is tapped into, overcoming any situation becomes easy. One way to ensure that you are persevering is to write down or speak into the existence your winning plan. This will ensure that you have the determination to win. Another thing to do is to target the end goal or the finish line which will focus your mind in one direction, opposed to many. Lastly, look up (yes, look at the sky from time to time.) because this will help shape your mind to think that your only vision path is higher than your current physical state. I love to look at the sky when I am recovering from a situation because it gives me the appropriate gas or fuel to elevate myself to the "what's next."

> **Point of Pride #13:** Energy is strength unused and unnoticed! Let that sink in for a moment.

Endurance:

This phenomenon or energy is rather big because whether you define it chemically, athletically, physiologically, or generally, there is one common theme: *the ability to overcome the opposition and achieve the desired end goal.* For example, to dive into the chemical correlation, when you place two compounds together that want to react (an electrophile and a nucleophile; acid and base; or a negatively charged species with a positively charged species, for example), sometimes in an unpleasant environment, the reaction still happens. The same can be athletes and how they display endurance. I love Cross-Fit because it is an interesting sport with built-in characteristics, one being that of endurance. During the middle or towards the end of an intense workout in Cross-Fit (which may include both weightlifting and cardio movements), that trait is the only energy that enables any athlete to finish the workout.

One may question, where does it come from and I believe the answer is, it depends on the source. That source is within you…in fact, it is in us all. Emphatically, the source can be anything such as past hurt, motivation, inspiration, desire, hunger to achieve, family pressure, and the list goes on. Again, one common underlying theme in all these cases mentioned (and the ones that are not) is "mindset." **In my opinion, endurance is a thought in your mind which requires energy and it provides stamina to "move on or up or out."** Opposed to taking a stimulant or drinking a caffeine source to gain that drive, endurance is like a natural stimulant that is derived from within YOU. Tapping into it will enable anyone to go against any force, win any situation, overcome any obstacle, and achieve every desire.

Can endurance be built, or does it genetically connect to you? The answer is complex, but I think it can be developed, however there may be some genetic connections. In sports, athletes train to build endurance to overcome a massive hit by another player (such as in American football), fatigue during distance (in running), and injury (in other various sports). So, when those events happen, it is less traumatic and overcoming it is easy. How is that related to us? Well, every life obstacle, learning lesson, situation, etc. is like our "training" and we go through it over the years. What you learn in high school sometimes is often revisited while you are in college. Endurance allows you to get through the phase. That was just a small classic example. As a child, we are trained on what is right or wrong, and the consequences are the true teachers. Throughout life, endurance is what follows perseverance and it is what will help you, as the individual, to move on. We must do one thing: *tap into it! This is an action!*

Effort:

To tap into it, however, requires effort! Though this word is a noun, it does relate to action. Effort is like that first walk as a child, going to high school on day 1, graduating from college to step into the real world, starting a new job, saying hello to that cute individual at a local spot, and other examples. Do you remember how you felt in any of those situations? Well, the feeling may have been like "just trying something out." On the flip side, once that first step is taken, it is over and cannot be replaced. Moving on is similar and having those elements (perseverance and endurance) mentioned in earlier sections are keys which leads to the effort. This is life changing, or can be, because it is new or different.

This only means that using effort will force you into a different phase, usually an elevated one. The scientific method and the data collected will all become important because it will force you to remember the items you identified, observations you made about your situation, testing that you fostered, and analysis. Each component will be the tools you will use to tap into your potential and overcoming your situation! A famous author, Eliezer Yudkowsky, said, "Trying and getting hurt can't possibly be worse for you than being... stuck." The author was conveying that in a stationary phase, where you are not mobile or are stuck, is not better than your attempt or effort even if it led you to being hurt. You took the first step! In the same sense, the use of effort instantly changes your situation from old to new. Ponder on this quote before moving on please.

> **Point of Pride #14:** Famous author Eliezer Yudkowsky, said, "Trying and getting hurt can't possibly be worse for you than being... stuck."

A Changed Mind:

What if you have those components -- perseverance, endurance, and effort -- but still have the same mindset, what will happen? The short answer is "nothing," and the longer answer is "you will waste your time." This will result in a temporary fix with a diagnosed problem. It is like, to use a medical phrase, putting a bandage over the problem. The bandage is not going to heal the wound…it just covers it up. A changed mindset is the vehicle which carries the other ingredients that you will use to go from your current state to your new state. It cannot be separated from the others and it is rather important to your situation, the scientific method approach, and your next step phase. In our brains, it is the center for controlling our thoughts, emotions, memory, speech, movement, and function of various organs. This means that everything for us as humans surrounds our mindset … it is our "king of the jungle." If it stays the same, depending on whether we are trying to get over an issue, master a skill, and other related situations mentioned throughout the book, NOTHING will change.

On the contrary, let's focus on when it changes and the result of that shift, which is paramount. The change explodes you into a new arena and mentality. Your actions (and words for the most part) will display that of someone else. Why? Your thinking will be different because you will have *a changed mind*. How you move, respond, assess, answer, and act will be new. Those changes will be the catalyst to employ your perseverance, endurance, and effort. And lastly, ***once the catalyst is activated and the other chemical reagents are present, a reaction begins which lead to a new product: your changed mindset.***

PART 4

Tying it all together.

Summary

This book was written during the first part of 2020, a year that brought us 2020 vision; COVID-19 (a virus) pandemic restructuring this world, and the loss of basketball legend Kobe Bryant in a helicopter crash (he was only 40 years old). In addition, locust appeared in East Africa, earthquakes rocked Turkey and the Caribbean, and American cities were the scenes of racial protests and riots. These listed are just a few events that took place by the time I was finished writing this book, I am sure more will happen because 2020 is proving to be a challenging year. The point of reference for all those things is 1) something happened, and it was identified, 2) a process or strategy was employed to solve some form of a problem to provide a solution, and 3) moving on took place. It is a part of our DNA and life to have a step-by-step periodic approach to all things; we are routine individuals that go by a process.

The essays from the first part of this book started out by displaying heart felt situations that touched on key points that we will all face and matters that are dear to my heart:

- fear
- family matters
- having courage
- overcoming trials
- being equipped to face a situation
- mindsets that will yield victory
- storms
- thinking like a lion
- roadblocks and re-directions
- and any other sub-topic you were able to pull out of the text…

Each were designed to do one major thing: identify the current state of mind I was in (or in general) which is the first step in any process. The phrase "2020" really stands for clarity and the two (identify and clarity) are cousins. They link because you must look at your situations with a clear perspective if you want to see the realness within it. Sometimes, this is our issue. Bias and a plethora of other items cloud our focus which then lead to cloudy results. One way to change that is, open your eyes and look in the mirror. By saying that, I am not only referring to a physical mirror, I am also referring to the mirror image of your reality. In the essay, "Fighting a Battle Un-Equipped," it was clear to me that your "effort must match your destination." This is a clear statement that means if you do not put 100% into "you," then your final stop/destination will only yield what you put into it. On the other hand, one must identify the effort or lack thereof so they can understand the result. This is key in realizing the type of weapons one chooses to fight with when in a battle; we will never live a life battle-free. However, how you step up for battle is dependent on YOU! Again, only **your eyes** can help you get to that point.

Do not lose focus of the topic of mindset throughout this book because it is at the forefront of your periodic process. If your mind is affected, blocked, trapped, and in danger, everything dealing with your brain is as well. ALL ABOARD! Having autonomy over your mind (meaning other people's action, your situation, and fear, just to name a few, cannot direct your mind) allows one to captain your own ship. When you give your mind room to be controlled, manipulated, and stimulated by other factors, you are not the owner. You are a renter and you are contracting out your residence in your mind. Why is this important? Ownership and renting are different in the sense that you have equity in one and no equity in the other. In your home as an owner, you can change the wall color, cut down a tree, renovate the basement, knock a wall down, purchase new appliances, add on to your property, or make any other improvements without the permission from anyone else. You make the ultimate decision. However, as a renter one must ask for consent to do any of the above (and in some cases you cannot do some of those items suggested because it is not your property). Own your mindset!

> **Point of Pride #15:** When you give your mind room to be controlled, manipulated, and stimulated by other factors, you are not the owner.

Fear is a mind killer! Not specifically, but some aspects of the essays touched on fear and its effects. It is a noun that does not receive much credit … it should be discussed more in detail or at least highlighted because it is a catastrophic emotion. It is like cancer or a deadly virus that can wipe out a generation of people, family, culture, and organization because it spreads and targets the mind. Fear within family (for example, abuse or divorce of parents which leads to their offspring not wanting to be in relationships); fear in business (for example, not wanting to invest or spend money because of bad financial decisions made in the past by others or you); fear within friendships (for example, a friend stop speaking to another because they got into an argument and no party thinks the other will change if they resolve it) can all lead to the end of family, business, and friendship relationships. As a result of that, I call it a mind-killer and a way to address it is to replace fear with courage. This is done by a process like the scientific method.

The scientific method is a true strategy that consist of key steps that will lead to the "what's next" phase. However, one must enjoy the process, even if it is raw and brutal. Each step has its own best-shared practices and key learnings that will add supplement to your growth and encourage you to keep moving to the next phase within the method. As stated earlier, process is inherited in our DNA (we do a lot of things periodically so we cannot run from it). It should be embraced because it is a way to overcome the many storms that we will face. Knowing the problem relates back to identify, designing your experiments helps you look at various correlations, analyzing the data ensures that what you are doing make sense (or not), and talking about your results enables a second opinion or at least an opportunity for you to hear out loud what you discovered about your solution to your problem. All of these are key to your what's next!

Moving on is like a mountain to the valley, a diamond to trash, sunlight to darkness, and a car to walking. It is the momentum that causes one to elevate, it is the difference. Everything that came before this moment determines this part. You cannot move on if you have not identified your mindset; if you are still renting your mind; allowing fear to determine your footsteps; and have not fostered a strategy to change. Moving on will more so look like "stuck!" To combat that, it only works when one accepts that they want newness. In my opinion, this is the hardest part, and it requires the most work. It is important to align every step of your process in a periodic fashion such as the scientific method and then move on to employ your nuggets mentioned earlier: perseverance, endurance, and effort. *They are reagents in your chemical reaction to yield a new product whether it is a new person, perspective, outlook, or outcome!*

_____

(Scientific Method Model Activity)

1. **Identify** your problem:

2. **Jot down** your thoughts about the situation (good or bad):

3. **Design** a set of key questions in a table or structured approach that you will need answers to that will help you assess the situation (example below):

#	Question/ concern/ thought	Answer/ comment
1		
2		

4. Once you have the answers, **analyze** them in respect to the questions that were asked, and your thoughts and the problem identified.

5. Make a **conclusion** about what you found, remember to remove the bias.

6. Create a plan of how your conclusion will move you on to the "what's next phase" or more so consider, **what is your next?**